P9-DGV-471

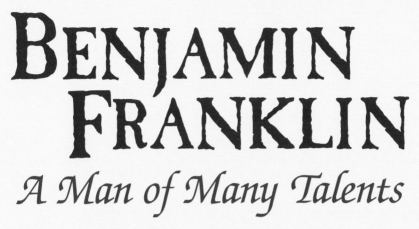

BENJAMIN FRANKLIN

A Man of Many Talents

By the Editors of TIME FOR KIDS
WITH KATHRYN HOFFMAN SATTERFIELD

■ **HarperCollins**Publishers

About the Author: Kathryn Hoffman Satterfield is an editor at TIME FOR KIDS®. In high school she portrayed Ben Franklin during history class debates. Since then she has been a great admirer of the inventor, writer, and patriot. The author is a proud resident of Brooklyn, New York.

Benjamin Franklin
Copyright © 2005 by Time Inc.
Used under exclusive license by HarperCollins Publishers Inc.
Manufactured in China by South China Printing Company Ltd.
All rights reserved. No part of this book may be used or reproduced in any manner whatsoever without written permission except in the case of brief quotations embodied in critical articles and reviews. For information address HarperCollins Children's Books, a division of HarperCollins Publishers, 1350 Avenue of the Americas, New York, NY 10019.
www.harperchildrens.com

Library of Congress Cataloging-in-Publication Data is available.
ISBN 0-06-057609-X (pbk). — ISBN 0-06-057610-3 (trade)

1 2 3 4 5 6 7 8 9 10
First Edition

Copyright © by Time Inc.

TIME FOR KIDS and the Red Border Design are Trademarks of Time Inc. used under license.

Photography and Illustration Credits:
Cover: artwork by Michael J. Deas; cover inset: Royalty-Free/Getty Images; cover flap: Bettmann/Corbis; p. iv: The Granger Collection; p.1: Royalty-Free/Getty Images; pp.2–3: The Granger Collection; p.4: Royalty-Free/Getty Images; p.5: Brown Brothers; p.6: The Granger Collection; p.7 (bottom left): The Granger Collection; p.7 (right): Bettmann/Corbis; p.8: The Granger Collection; p.9: The Granger Collection (2); p.10: The Granger Collection; p.11: The Granger Collection; p.12: The Granger Collection; p.13 (bottom): North Wind Archives/North Wind Production; p.14: The Granger Collection; p.15: The Granger Collection; pp.16–17: The Granger Collection (3); p.18: The Granger Collection; p.19: Bettmann/Corbis; p.20: American Philosophical Society; p.21: The Granger Collection; p.22: The Granger Collection; p.23: The Granger Collection; p.24: Bettmann/Corbis; p.25 (top left): Lee Snider; Lee Snider/Corbis; p.25 (middle): The Granger Collection; p.25 (bottom): North Wind Archives/North Wind Production; p.26 (top): Culver Pictures; p.26 (bottom): Lee Snider; Lee Snider/Corbis; p.27: The Granger Collection; p.28 (top): The Granger Collection; p.28 (bottom): Time Life Picture Collection; p.29: Brown Brothers; p.30: The Granger Collection; p.31 (top & bottom): Bettmann/Corbis; p.32: The Granger Collection; p.33 (top & bottom): The Granger Collection; p.34 (top): Library of Congress; p.34 (bottom): The Granger Collection; p.35: The Granger Collection; p.36: The Granger Collection; p.37 (top): The Granger Collection; p.37 (bottom left): Corbis; p.38: Brown Brothers; p.39 (top & bottom): Bettmann/Corbis; p.40: Bettmann/Corbis; p. 41 (top): Royalty-Free/Getty Images; p.41 (bottom left): Kevin Fleming/Corbis; p.41 (bottom right): The Granger Collection; p.42: Time Life Picture Collection; p.43 (top): Ron Sachs/Corbis; p.43 (bottom): Royalty-Free/Corbis; p.44 (top left): North Wind Archives/North Wind Production; p.44 (top right): Royalty-Free/Getty Images; p.44 (second on right): The Granger Collection; p.44 (bottom right): Royalty-Free/Getty Images; back cover: The Granger Collection.

Acknowledgments:
For TIME FOR KIDS: Editorial Director: Keith Garton; Editor: Jonathan Rosenbloom; Art Director: Rachel Smith; Designer: Colleen Pidel; Photography Editor: Sandy Perez; Contributing Editor: Elaine Israel

HarperCollins books may be purchased for educational, business, or sales promotional use. For information, please write: Special Markets Department, HarperCollins Publishers Inc., 10 East 53rd Street, New York, NY 10022.

 **Find out more at www.timeforkids.com/bio/franklin**

Curr
E
302.6
.F8
B4525
2005

CONTENTS

> "Well done is better than well said."
> —BEN FRANKLIN

▶ BEN'S KITE experiment proved that lightning is electricity. This drawing shows Ben with his son, William.

Chapter One

Sparks

FLY

*T*he skies that June day in 1752 were dark and stormy in Philadelphia. Most people stayed inside their homes to keep dry. But not Benjamin Franklin.

There he stood in the wind, the rain, and the lightning. And he was flying a kite!

It was not just any kite. Ben had placed a metal wire at the top of the kite and a metal key at the end of the string he held. His son, William, stood at his side as a bolt of lightning shot through the air. It hit the metal wire. A spark flew. It traveled

◄ ELECTRICITY from lightning flowed from Ben's kite to a key.

▲ ELECTRICITY fascinated Ben. He performed many experiments to see how it worked.

down the string to the key. Ben put his knuckle to the key and felt a jolt. Success! He had just proved that lightning was electricity.

To Ben, this experiment was one of his "electrical amusements." It was both dangerous and fun. But it was also very important. For one thing, his experiment led to his invention of the lightning rod. This gadget still saves many buildings from burning today.

Who was Benjamin Franklin? He was a plainly dressed, rather chubby man with eyes that twinkled

(from behind the bifocal glasses he invented). His mind was always spinning and he was always thinking up new ideas. He was honored by kings and by shopkeepers alike. Ben's ideas were so practical that most are still in use after more than two hundred years. How did a scruffy boy from a colonial city grow up to be such an amazing man of the world?

◄ **SHOCKING!**
Franklin invented the lightning rod—a long piece of metal that sits on the roof and runs into the ground. Lightning is drawn to the rod rather than to the house.

Chapter Two

Books

AND DREAMS

*B*enjamin Franklin was born in Boston, Massachusetts, on January 17, 1706. (Massachusetts was one of the thirteen colonies ruled by Britain. It was in a part of the country called New England.) Ben was the third youngest of seventeen children. It must have been hard to be a quiet child living with a big, noisy family. But it didn't seem to bother Ben.

By the age of seven, he had taught himself to read and write. Some of the books he read belonged to his family. Others were borrowed from neighbors. His father, Josiah, always found

▲ THE GOOD BOOK
In colonial times, most families owned and read the Bible.

▲ AN ARTIST drew this picture of Benjamin Franklin as a young boy.

time to talk with Ben about whatever he was reading.

Sometimes Ben read through much of the night. During the day he helped his father make candles and soap in the family's shop. He often daydreamed of boarding one of the ships in busy Boston Harbor and sailing to places far away.

Ben Goes to School

Josiah and his wife, Abiah, wanted the best for their smart young son. When Ben was about eight years old,

▲ **MOST KIDS** went to one-room schools like this one.

his parents sent him to a famous school, the Boston Latin School. They hoped he would one day become a church minister. Ben was one of the school's best students. But Ben's parents soon realized that their son was not meant to be a church minister. They thought he was just too active for church life. So they took Ben out of school after two years. It was back to the candle shop for him.

That didn't mean his education was over. For Ben, everything—big or small—was worth learning about. And he was always interested in figuring out how something worked or could be made better.

The waters of Boston Harbor and the

Charles River were great places for Ben to learn new things. There Ben taught himself to swim. But, being Ben, he wanted to swim faster. So he made two paddles for his hands. He made flippers for his feet. He invented swim fins and became a speedy swimmer—and an inventor!

▼ **DIVE RIGHT IN!**
Ben learned how to swim in the waters of Boston Harbor.

FAST FACTS
Kids in Colonial Times

☛ Colonial times were tough. There was no electricity. And there were no children's books! Kids read the Bible, books about manners, and adult stories.

☛ Boys and girls worked hard. Kids got up early before school to do chores. After school they went back to work. They helped to garden, feed animals, cook, and clean.

☛ Young children went to school to learn to read and write. Boys kept learning after that. Girls stayed home and learned to cook and sew.

☛ Most toys were homemade. Boys may have played with toy houses made from corncobs. Girls played with cornhusk dolls.

Chapter Three

A BOY NAMED
Silence

The Franklins realized that Ben should learn another trade besides making candles. When he was twelve, Ben was sent to live with his older brother James to learn the job of printing. The plan was for Ben to train for seven years. Then he would open his own print shop.

In the colonies news was spread by newspapers and booklets because there was no television, radio, or

◀ **AS A BOY,** Ben took a beginner's job in a print shop.

▶ **PRINT SHOPS** in the 1700s looked much like this one. The machine in the photo printed the papers.

Internet. Printers were important and respected people. James owned a newspaper, *The New England Courant*. It carried some news stories and advertisements. But mostly it was known for its articles written by people with strong opinions.

New England had been settled by Puritans looking for religious freedom. But the Puritans weren't always open to new ideas. They wanted everyone to share their beliefs. As for the British rulers, they mostly left the colonials alone. But they kept a sharp eye on what was written.

◀ **SPREAD THE NEWS!** Ben's brother James owned *The New England Courant*. This issue was published in 1723.

▶ TURNING a printing press took a great deal of strength.

To protect themselves, writers used fake names. That way they felt free to say what they wanted. This world of printing was filled with rebels and new ideas. It was the perfect world for Ben.

James taught Ben how to use the press to print the paper. Ben also wrote some poems that he didn't think were very good, but his brother liked them and published them. However, James would not accept any serious work from Ben. After all, James thought his brother was just a little boy who had never even left Boston. What could he know?

All his life Ben had liked to play tricks on people. This time he played one on James. Ben created a character called Mrs. Silence Dogood. He wrote fourteen articles under that name. He even changed his handwriting so James wouldn't know he'd written them. Late at night Ben would slip the essays under the door of James's print shop.

Silence was a widow who lived out in the country. She was far from silent, though. (That was one of Ben's little jokes.) Silence had strong

▶ **JAMES FRANKLIN** sometimes took out his anger on brother Ben.

▶ HOT OFF THE PRESS! The articles Ben wrote for his brother's newspaper were very popular.

opinions and wrote in a sharp, funny way. She criticized people who told others how to think and act. Silence said politics should be kept separate from religion. But Silence's articles weren't all critical. She also wrote about her love for her country.

Silence Dogood was a hit with the paper's readers. Ben later let on that he was Silence Dogood. This surprised many people, including his family.

Ben had strong opinions and spoke his mind. James had a bad temper. The two did not always get

along. So, when
Ben was
seventeen, he
decided to
move on. One
of his dreams
was about to
come true. He
was leaving
Boston for good.

The Thirteen
COLONIES

The original thirteen
colonies were all in the
eastern part of what is now
the United States. By the
1700s the colonies belonged
to Britain, which sent
representatives of the king to
rule. The colonies are listed
below in the order that the
first permanent white settlers
moved there.

Virginia — 1607
New Jersey — 1618
Massachusetts — 1620
New Hampshire — 1622
Pennsylvania — 1623
New York — 1624
Maryland — 1634
Connecticut — 1635
Rhode Island — 1636
Delaware — 1638
North Carolina — 1653
South Carolina — 1670
Georgia — 1733

Chapter Four

Home
AWAY FROM HOME

*B*en headed for Philadelphia, Pennsylvania, in 1723. The cobblestone streets there were filled with carriages, carts, horses, and people. Ben knew this lively city was just the place for him.

He had arrived in Philadelphia dirty, hungry, and broke. But he quickly found a job at a printing shop. His personality and skills made a good impression on everyone he

◄ **SIR WILLIAM KEITH** was the governor of Pennsylvania from 1716 to 1726. The governor broke his promise to Ben.

14

▲ **THE NAME PHILADELPHIA** comes from the Greek words for "brother" and "love." So it's known as the "City of Brotherly Love."

met. Sir William Keith, the British governor of Pennsylvania, even offered to help Ben start his own printing business. He said that Ben should go to London, England, to buy supplies. When he arrived in London, there would be money waiting for him.

Out of Luck

Another dream came true for Ben. He sailed across the Atlantic Ocean and arrived in London on Christmas Eve, 1724. It was so exciting! Ben had never seen so many people rushing about. The street sounds startled him. The strange smells made him dizzy.

Chapter Five

TAKING CARE OF

Business

▲ NOT ONLY DID BEN PRINT
The Pennsylvania Gazette, he
wrote all its articles.

*S*hortly after returning
from London, Ben
opened his own printing
shop. Then in 1729, he
started a newspaper, *The
Pennsylvania Gazette.* At
first, he was the paper's
only worker. He was the
reporter, the editor, the
typesetter, and the
business manager.

Ben had a nose for
news. He also wrote silly
stories that made readers
laugh. Before long, the *Gazette*

▲ **A BUSY WORKER** delivers paper to print *The Pennsylvania Gazette*.

became the largest newspaper in America.

The printing business, too, did very well. Ben became the official printer of Pennsylvania. He printed money, documents, and booklets for the colony. Then he became the printer for Delaware, New Jersey, and Maryland. He ran his printing business until 1748.

Ben and Deborah

Life for Ben wasn't all work and no play. One of his first friends in Philadelphia was Deborah Read. When

◀ A PARTNER FOR LIFE
Deborah Read had two children with Ben.
She also helped run their businesses.

she first saw Ben in 1723, she thought he was very messy and noticed that his clothes were dirty. Deborah probably never imagined that seven years later, she and Ben would be together for the rest of her life.

But that's just what happened. When Ben returned from London, he had enough money to afford marriage. He wanted to marry Deborah.

There were some problems, though. Ben had a baby son, William. (The name of the boy's mother was a well-kept secret.) And Deborah had a husband, John Rogers. He had left her. She didn't know if he was dead or alive.

As long as she was still married to John, Deborah couldn't marry again. So in 1730 she and Ben decided to live together. She took in William and had two

▶ BEN CALLED DEBORAH a "good and faithful helpmate."
They worked to make each other happy.

Happiness.— That to secure these rights, Governments are instituted among
destructive of these ends it is the Right of the People to alter or to abolish it.

children with Ben. Francis, their son, died when he
was five of smallpox, a terrible and common disease.
Their daughter, Sarah, known as Sally, lived a long life.

Deborah and Ben were great partners. Deborah
was afraid to sail on the ocean and watched over
their businesses when Ben was away. She wrote him
loving letters filled with news and gossip, which he
eagerly read.

interrupt our connections and correspondence. They too have been deaf to
tion, and hold them as we hold the rest of mankind, Enemies in War, in

Chapter Six

THE GOOD
Citizen

*B*en never forgot that he came from a hard-working family. He felt most at home with "middling," or ordinary, people. But he was interested in everyone, no matter what the person's religion or where the person came from. He believed that citizens should always help one another.

Those feelings were possibly the reason he started a club called Junto. Its

◀ BEN FRANKLIN and the members of the Junto club started the nation's first public library.

▶ BOOKWORM
Ben liked to read and discuss ideas with his Junto friends.

first twelve members were people who Ben thought were smart and interesting, with great ideas to help improve people's lives. The members included some of his friends, merchants, craftsmen, a mathematician, and an astrologer. They talked about books, politics, and current events. The group met on Friday nights and shared long candlelit dinners of applewood-smoked pork chops at the City Tavern. If a member got angry at something another member said, he would have to pay a small but embarrassing fine. This way members could speak their minds and all ideas were treated with respect. Even Ben had to pay a fine if he stepped out of line.

But the group's main purpose was to do good works for others. Ben had always loved to read, so his club helped start the first free public library in North America. The Library Company of

Ben's Great IDEAS

Ben Franklin was famous for his many inventions and new ideas. Here are a few of them.

Armonica: Different thicknesses of glass made different sounds in this musical instrument. Beethoven and Mozart, two famous composers, both wrote special music for it.

Bifocals: People wore these glasses to read and to see distances at the same time.

Gulf Stream: Franklin mapped the Gulf Stream. This is the name for the powerful currents in the Atlantic Ocean.

▲ SWEET SOUNDS
Ben loved to play his armonica.

Philadelphia opened in 1731. Before then libraries were private. Only rich people could borrow books from them. Now everyone could.

& INVENTIONS

JOIN, or DIE.

☞ **Odometer:** An odometer keeps track of the distance a vehicle travels. Franklin invented one for his carriage.

☞ **Franklin stove:** People could heat their homes with this iron furnace stove. It used less wood and was safer than other types of stoves.

☞ **Daylight saving time:** Ben thought it was a good idea to move the clocks ahead by one hour in the summer. This would make it possible for people to have more hours of daylight to work when the weather was warm.

BEN'S OPINION ►
This is Ben's first and most famous political cartoon.

☞ **Political cartoon:** Franklin is given credit for being the first person to feature a cartoon with a point of view about a current event. It appeared in *The Pennsylvania Gazette*.

◄ HOT IDEA
The Franklin stove made heating homes safer and cheaper.

◄ **THE JUNTO CLUB** helped form a volunteer fire department for Philadelphia. Here's Ben wearing a firefighter's hat.

Fire It Up!

The club did something else to help the people of Philadelphia. It started the city's first volunteer fire department. The city had many wooden houses. Everyone used candles. The firefighters and their horse-drawn wagons were kept busy putting out flames, making Philadelphia safer.

Ben also decided to offer fire insurance to homeowners. He had picked up the idea for this insurance while in London. People strolling along Philadelphia's Elfreth's Alley would see black iron signs on some of the houses. The signs showed that the houses

◄ **A ROW HOUSE**, built in the 1700s, stands on Elfreth's Alley.

had fire insurance. It was an early form of advertising.

Elfreth's Alley featured another of Ben's inventions. Tiny mirrors were hung outside windows on upper floors. They let people inside watch who was coming and going in the alley. No wonder they were called busybody mirrors!

The members of Junto also started a school that became the University of Pennsylvania. In addition the club formed the first public hospital and a

▲ FIRES SPREAD QUICKLY through the wooden houses of colonial Philadelphia.

police department. Junto lasted for forty years. Some of its members went on to start other clubs to do good works for people.

Words to Live By

Ben had a rule that said, "Early to bed, early to rise, makes a man healthy, wealthy, and wise." Even while being an inventor, traveler, scientist, citizen, husband, father, and printer, Ben still found time for some other activities.

He was elected to the Pennsylvania Assembly, which made laws for the colony. He also became the head of Philadelphia's post office. In 1753 the British put him in charge of the entire mail system for all the colonies. In those days mail delivery wasn't regular.

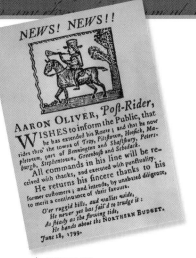

▲ HIRE ME!
In this ad, a man offers to deliver mail by horseback.

Sometimes the mail arrived. And sometimes it didn't. Ben changed that. He even set up the first home-delivery system.

Through his job, Ben came into contact with people from all over the East Coast. This helped him better understand what the colonists were worried about and what they thought of

◀ BEN BELIEVED hard work was good for a person. He worked at many tasks his whole life.

their government. Ben listened carefully to what people had to say. He heard their ideas and their different points of view about being ruled by Britain— and he thought about what he was hearing.

► THANKS TO BEN, mail service throughout the American colonies was improved. Here, mail is being delivered by boat.

Chapter Seven

BEN'S GREAT
Adventure

*A*lthough Ben worked for the British, he didn't agree with everything they did. Ben was soon involved in the greatest adventure of his life.

In the 1750s the British fought—and won—a long and expensive war against France. To pay for the French and Indian War, the British decided to heavily tax the colonists.

◄A LIFE IN POLITICS
Starting in 1751, Ben served as a public official for almost forty years.

► **KING GEORGE III** of England wanted to keep tight control over his American colonies.

(A tax is a government charge, or fee, on products.) The colonists, of course, were not happy about this.

In 1757 Ben once again went to London. This time he was sent by the Pennsylvania Assembly. Could he convince the British to drop the taxes?

William went with his father. Both were hopeful that the problems could be worked out. Ben met with King George III and other officials. He returned home to Deborah and Sally five years later, feeling pleased. But that feeling didn't last long. The troubles between Britain and the colonies got worse.

▲ **THE BRITISH** defeated France in the French and Indian War. The British taxed the colonies to pay for the war.

▲ **ANGRY CITIZENS** of Boston read the news about the Stamp Act.

Stamp Out the Stamp Act

In 1765 the British passed the Stamp Act. The Stamp Act was a tax on all printed material in the colonies—books, newspapers, pamphlets, even playing cards. The British taxed the colonists without asking them. This made the colonists very angry. Riots broke out in some of the colonies.

Ben was against the Stamp Act. He went back to London and spoke before Parliament, which makes the laws for Britain. The lawmakers listened and dropped the tax. Ben stayed in England to give the colonists' point of view on other issues as well. But the

An Emblem of the Effects of the STAMP
O! the fatal Stamp.

◀ A CARTOON from 1765 attacks the Stamp Act.

British weren't willing to give in to the colonists on all things. In fact, in 1774 the British government decided to send soldiers to control the angry Americans.

Ben was still in London when Deborah died in 1774. She had suffered a stroke. She died in the large house they had built so proudly eight years before.

Feeling sad about Deborah's death, Ben wanted to return to America. But there was another reason why Ben wanted to leave England. He had hoped that the British and the colonists could work out their problems. Now he realized that this was not going to happen. Ben knew it was time to take a stand for his country.

▲ BEN told the British lawmakers that the Stamp Act was unfair. He won the argument!

War Begins

The American Revolution began on April 19, 1775. Ben arrived home two weeks later. He was made a member of the Second Continental Congress. It had members from each of the colonies. At age sixty-nine, he was the oldest delegate.

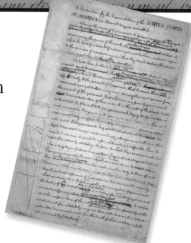

▲ **MANY CHANGES** were made to the Declaration of Independence before it was approved.

America should be free from Britain, Ben said. On his own, he wrote his reasons for becoming independent. Slowly others in the Congress

began to agree with him. In 1776 Ben joined four other lawmakers to create the Declaration of Independence. Thomas Jefferson wrote it. Ben made some changes to the wording.

On July 4, 1776, the Declaration was approved by the Congress. This wasn't done lightly. The British would say the signers were traitors. Ben urged the signing, saying, "We must all hang together, or assuredly we shall all hang separately." He knew it was important to stand together and to fight together for independence.

◄ THE DECLARATION of Independence was created mainly by Franklin, Jefferson, John Adams, Robert Livingston, and Roger Sherman.

☞ CLUE 1: I was born in 1743 in Virginia and became the third president of the United States in 1801.

☞ CLUE 2: My home, called Monticello, features many of my inventions, including a special kind of sundial to tell time.

☞ CLUE 3: I nearly doubled the size of the United States after I approved the Louisiana Purchase in 1803.

Who am I?

ANSWER: THOMAS JEFFERSON

▲ **KING LOUIS XVI AND QUEEN MARIE ANTOINETTE** met with Ben in Paris, France.

Ben Goes to France

On the war front, the American army struggled. It needed money, supplies, and trained officers. The Continental Congress asked Ben to go to France and ask for help. Ben was ill. He knew the voyage would be long. But he went anyway to help his country.

Ben arrived in Paris, France, in December 1776. He met the French king and queen. Important French officials greeted him. They wore the popular style of the day—great powdered wigs, fancy clothes, jewels, and even pointy shoes with high heels. Ben wore an old fur cap and a brown wool suit. He knew this would get their attention. And it did.

This elderly man, who cared so deeply about his

young nation, was very appealing. He spoke of America simply and honestly. Women wrote him poems and fell in love with him. His picture was placed on rings, handkerchiefs, and medals. He was treated like a hero wherever he went.

▲ WOMEN loved Ben's fur hat. It was simple compared to the fancy hats of the time.

Still the French took their time joining America's fight. On February 6, 1778, they at last signed the Treaty of Alliance and agreed to help. The French sent much-needed money, troops, ships, and weapons to America.

Three years later the British surrendered at the Battle of Yorktown in Virginia. The American Revolution ended in October 1781.

Ben stayed in France to help create a peace treaty between America and Britain. When he signed the Treaty of Paris for the United States in 1783, he was overjoyed. At age seventy-seven, Ben had helped his nation to be born.

◄ THE TREATY OF PARIS was signed by Franklin, John Adams, and others. It ended the American Revolution.

Chapter Eight

Home
FOR GOOD

*I*n 1785 Ben returned to Philadelphia for good. He had been away for nine years. A cheering crowd welcomed him home. His daughter, Sally, hugged him tightly. His son, William, who had supported the British during the war, was not there to greet him.

Ben continued to serve his country. In 1787 he joined the Constitutional Convention. He helped to write the Constitution on which our laws are based. Others who

◄ **ARRIVING HOME from France in 1785, Ben was treated as a hero.**

> ▶ **GEORGE WASHINGTON** led the Constitutional Convention. But Ben's humor, calmness, and good sense helped get all the delegates to sign the Constitution.

worked on the Constitution had strong ideas that they would not give up. Ben came up with a plan that made just about everyone happy.

Benjamin Franklin died on April 17, 1790, in Philadelphia, at the age of eighty-four. Twenty thousand people attended his funeral. Marching behind his casket were all of the

▶ **BEN WORKED HARD** to get the colonies to approve the Constitution.

We the People

◄ **BENJAMIN FRANKLIN** was a great statesman, scientist, writer, and thinker.

clergymen in Philadelphia. Quakers, Protestants, Catholics, and Jews were among them.

No matter what their beliefs, Americans of all faiths and from all walks of life came out to honor this amazing man. They knew that Ben was a special person whom history would never forget.

Benjamin Franklin would still be remembered today, even if his only inventions had been bifocal eyeglasses, swim fins, and lightning rods. Even if he had only created free libraries, fire departments, insurance companies, and better post offices, Ben's name would still be known.

But Benjamin Franklin did more than come up with inventions, start up businesses and services, and serve in government. He helped to *create* a government—the government of the United States of America. This creation, which he worked so hard for and believed in so deeply, towers above all his other works.

Thanks in part to his great mind, and the fact that he could get people to agree on issues, the United States remains a powerful, independent democracy today.

▼ **FRANKLIN'S grave is in Philadelphia.**

Ben's Birdbrained IDEA

In 1782 Congress chose the bald eagle as America's national symbol. Ben thought the turkey would be better. He called the bald eagle a bird of "bad moral character." But the turkey, he said, was a "true, original native of America."

Here are some other symbols of the United States:

☞ Liberty Bell Philadelphia (1753)

☞ Washington Monument Washington, D.C. (1885)

☞ Statue of Liberty New York City (1886)

TALKING ABOUT
Franklin

▲ **Walter Isaacson**

TIME FOR KIDS editor Kathryn Hoffman Satterfield spoke with Walter Isaacson about Benjamin Franklin. His carefully researched book *Benjamin Franklin* was a best-seller.

Q. *If Benjamin Franklin were alive today, what might he think of our politics?*

A. He would believe that people should try to find common ground because we share certain values. He might say, "Let's see what works and let's be practical."

Q. *Do you think Ben would recognize today's government as the one he helped to create?*

A. Yes. He would appreciate that we're still a strong

◀ **BEN'S WORK HELPED** make the United States a great democracy.

democracy that protects the liberties of each of its citizens.

Q. *In your opinion, what are his most important contributions to society?*

A. As a scientist, he showed that electricity flows. From that he created the most important invention of his time, the lightning rod.

As a public citizen, his most important contribution was that the foundation of our communities would be voluntary civic associations—schools, libraries, volunteer fire corps. He was always good at helping people work together—and getting them to come together and agree on things.

▶ **MODERN FIREFIGHTERS** can thank Ben Franklin for having begun a volunteer fire department.

Benjamin Franklin's KEY DATES

1706	Born on January 17, in Boston, Massachusetts
1718	Trains with his brother James as a printer
1728	Opens his own print shop in Philadelphia
1732	Publishes the first edition of *Poor Richard's Almanack*; forms a volunteer fire brigade; becomes Philadelphia postmaster
1752	Conducts lightning experiment
1776	Elected to Second Continental Congress; goes to France
1787	Helps write the Constitution
1790	Dies on April 17, in Philadelphia, Pennsylvania

1709 The piano is invented.

1785 American colonists begin to sing "Yankee Doodle."

1789 The French Revolution begins.